Sally

Lehrwerk für den
Englischunterricht ab Klasse 1

Activity Book 3
Förderheft

Erarbeitet von
Jasmin Brune, Daniela Elsner, Stefanie Gleixner-Weyrauch,
Simone Gutwerk, Martina Koch, Marion Lugauer, Sabine Schwarz

Auf der Grundlage der Ausgabe von
Martina Bredenbröcker, Jasmin Brune, Daniela Elsner,
Barbara Gleich, Stefanie Gleixner-Weyrauch, Simone Gutwerk,
Marion Lugauer, Sabine Schwarz, Anke Spangenberg

Unter Beratung von Jane Brockmann-Fairchild

Portfolio: Nina Thelen

Illustriert von
Barbara Jung, Wilfried Poll, Anja Boretzki,
Thilo Pustlauk, Gisela Vogel

 Deine **interaktiven Gratis-Übungen** findest du hier:

1. Gehe auf scook.de.
2. Gib den unten stehenden Zugangscode in die Box ein.
3. Hab viel Spaß mit deinen Gratis-Übungen.

Dein Zugangscode auf
www.scook.de

Die Gratis-Übungen können dort
nach Bestätigung der allgemeinen
Geschäftsbedingungen genutzt werden.

r3d6t-tekk6

Oldenbourg Schulbuchverlag, München

P110373 BS_CV-Sally2 Ed.2 01 Kap 01 Kl...

Inhalt

Hello 3

Colours and numbers 5

At school 7

Body and feelings 9

Toys 13

Clothes 15

Weather and days 17

Around the year 20

Family and friends 22

Drinks 25

Breakfast 26

Fruit 28

Pets 31

London 34

Farm animals 36

Summer 37

Robin Hood 38

Special days:

Happy Halloween 39

Merry Christmas 40

Happy Easter 42

Dialogues 44

Board game 46

Schneidebogen 47

How are you?

1 🖊️✏️ **Draw a picture of yourself or stick in a photo.**

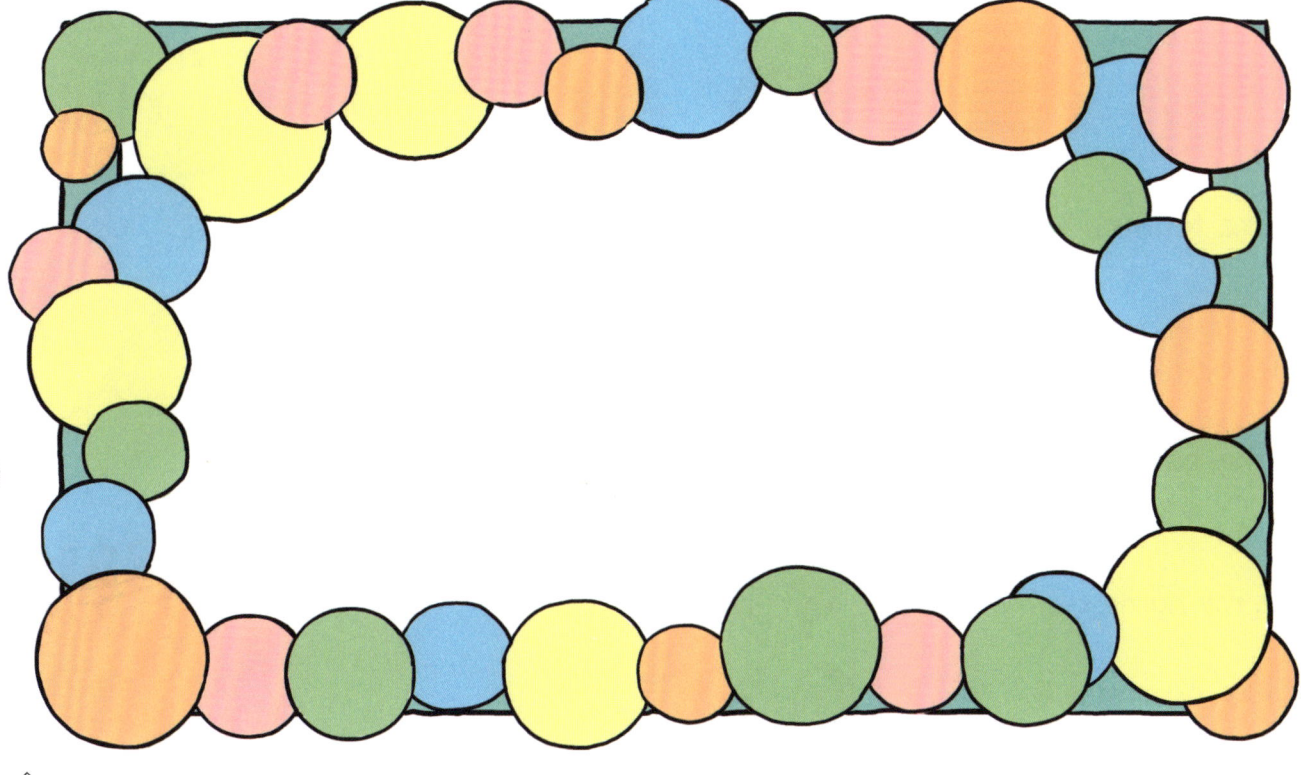

🖊️ Hi, my name is _____ .

2 🖊️ **Read and write.**

Hello, my name is Sally.
What's your name?

How are you?

My name is
_____ .

I'm fine, thank you.

Sally 3 Activity Book Förderheft (Englisch ab Klasse 1) © 2017 Cornelsen Verlag GmbH, Berlin

Who is it?

1 💿 **Listen.**

2 ✏️ **Draw lines and write.**

Hi, I'm Susan.

I like **tennis**.

Hello, my name is Tim.

I like **computer games**.

Hi, my name is Phil.

I like **basketball**.

Good morning, I'm Eric.

I like my **skateboard**.

Hello, I'm Emily.

I like **singing**.

Hi, my name is Liz.

I like **inline skating**.

3 ✏️ **Fill in your portfolio.**

Hello, I'm Sally and I ♥ lollipops.

💬 **And you?**
What do you like?

What colour is it?

1  **Colour and write.**

g r e e n   o r a n g e   p i n k

g r e y   p u r p l e   b r o w n

2   **Listen to the song and colour. Write the text.**

⬡ + ⬡ , ⬡ + ⬡ , ⬡ + ⬡ . (2 x)

Red and yellow, blue and green, blue and green.

And ⬡ + ⬡ + ⬡ + ⬡ .

And brown and black and white and grey.

⬡ + ⬡ , ⬡ + ⬡ , ⬡ + ⬡ .

R_____ and y_____ , b_____ and g_____ , b_____ and g_____ .

Ten kangaroos

1 ✏️ Draw lines.

2 💿 ✏️ Listen and colour.

seven

ten

one   eight

                six

two   three

five   nine

                four

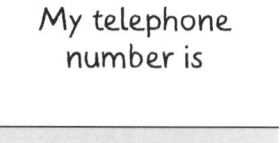

What's your telephone number?

> My telephone number is
>
> _____ .

3 💿 ✏️ Listen and write.

Emily

9	8		

Tim and Susan

Phil

4 🐾 Make a telephone list. Ask your friends.

⭐ Do you know other important telephone numbers?

police …
school …
Grandma …
Mum's mobile …

5 ✏️ Fill in your portfolio.

Sally 3 Activity Book Förderheft / Englisch ab Klasse 1) © 2017 Cornelsen Verlag GmbH, Berlin

School things

1 🖊 **Number and write.**

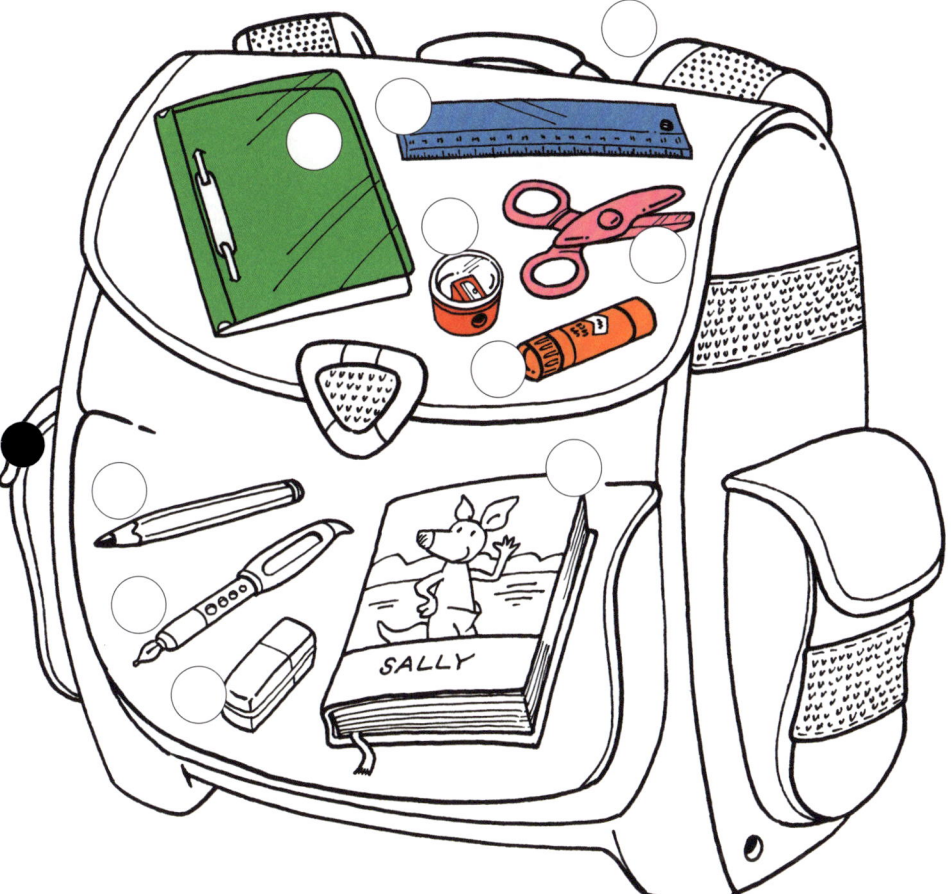

1 ruler

2 folder

3 glue stick

4 scissors

5 pencil sharpener

6 **rubber**

7 **pencil**

8 **pen**

9 **book**

10 **schoolbag**

2 ✏ **Colour the pictures.**

3 👦👧 **Tell your partner:** My ruler is blue.

4 🖊 **Do the crossword.**

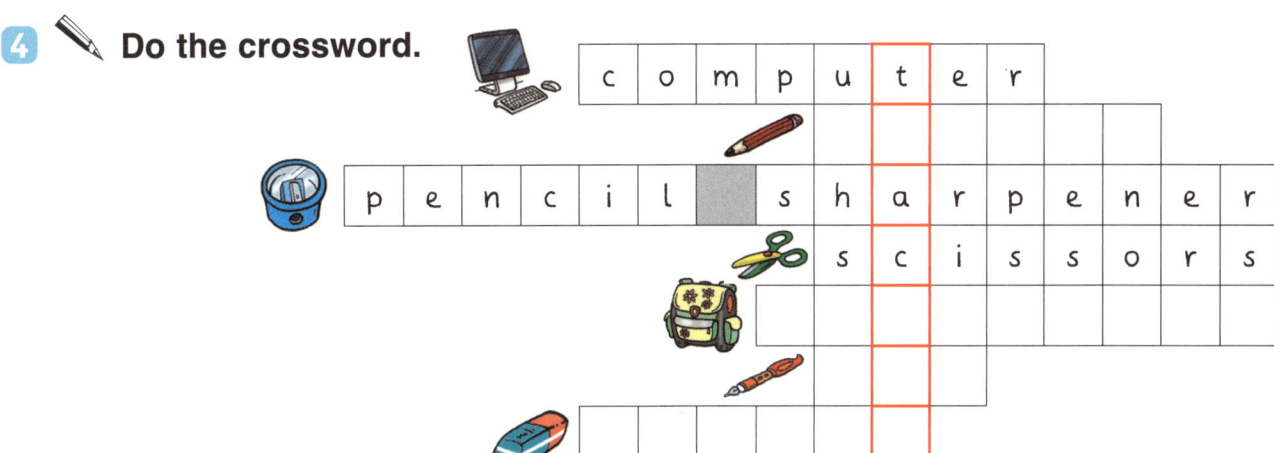

The word is: t _ _ _ _ _ _

Sally 3 Activity Book Förderheft (Englisch ab Klasse 1) © 2017 Cornelsen Verlag GmbH, Berlin

At school

Where are the school things?

1 ✏️ **Read and draw lines.**

The pencil case is **under** the schoolbag.

The rubber is **in** the pencil case.

The glue stick is **on** the book.

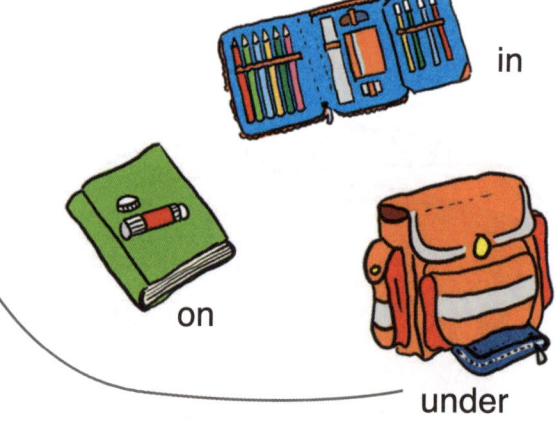 in

on

under

2 ✂️ **Read and draw.**

The pencil is **on** the book.   The ruler is **under** the folder.

3 ✏️ **Look at the pictures and write.**

The book is _____ the schoolbag.   The ruler is _____ the schoolbag.

4 ✏️✂️ **Write and colour.**

The book is _____

the _____.

5 ✏️ **Fill in your portfolio.**

Sally 3 Activity Book Förderheft (Englisch ab Klasse 1) © 2017 Cornelsen Verlag GmbH, Berlin

The body

1 ✏️ **Number and write.**

○ knees   ○ eyes

○ toes   ① ears

○ shoulders   ○ head

○ mouth   ○ nose

Ouch!

2 🦘 **Write your own comic. Act it out.**

Good morning, Sally.
Here is your tea.

I can't go to school.

Ouch! My
_____.

Let me see.

Ouch! My
_____.

Let me see.

Go to school.

 **Body and feelings**

Get up, Susan!

1  Listen.

2 Write the words.

3 Cut out the pictures (page 47), match and stick in.

Stretch your arms.

Stretch your legs.

Shake your hands.

Shake your fingers.

Shake your feet.

Go into the bathroom.

Wash your face.

Brush your hair.

Brush your teeth.

Open your mouth.

Say: Good morning!

1 arm – 2 arms
1 leg – 2 legs

1 foot – 2 feet
1 tooth – 2 teeth

Sally 3 Activity Book Förderheft (Englisch ab Klasse 1) © 2017 Cornelsen Verlag GmbH, Berlin

Monster, monster, how do you feel?

1 ✏️ **Look and write.**

The monster is _____ .

The monster is tired .

The monster is scared .

The monster is _____ .

sad   angry   ~~scared~~
fine   happy   ~~tired~~   okay

_____

And I feel **fine**!

2 ✏️ **How do you feel? Write.**

I'm _____ .

If you're happy

1. If you're hap – py and you know it, clap your hands.

If you're hap – py and you know it, clap your hands.

If you're hap – py and you know it and you real – ly want to show it,

if you're hap – py and you know it, clap your hands.

1 🖊 **Listen and write.**

2 🖊 **Draw lines.**

If you're happy and you know it,

       clap your hands ...

       stamp your feet ...

       snap your fingers ...

       say: we are ...

       do it all ...

3 🖊 **Now it's your turn. Write.**

If you're _____ and you know it,

angry   scared

sad   tired

4 🖊 **Fill in your portfolio.**

Sally 3 Activity Book Förderheft (Englisch ab Klasse 1) © 2017 Cornelsen Verlag GmbH, Berlin

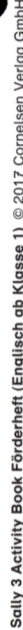

The fish who could wish

1  **Listen and tick ✔. Write the words.**

castle

car

doll

helicopter

horse

computer
game

guitar

teddy bear

2 **Now it's your turn. What do you wish for? Write or draw.**

bike   skateboard   computer
football   book …

Sally 3 Activity Book Förderheft (Englisch ab Klasse 1) © 2017 Cornelsen Verlag GmbH, Berlin

What can the children buy?

£80
£10
castle
doll
£20 helicopter
spaceship
£17
£18
football
£8
£30
racing car
helmet
£90 bike
rubber
book
helmet
£1
£5
£40
£2
£3
bike
ruler
pencils
£100
£ 200

£10
+£5
+£2
+£2
+£1
=£20

£10
+£2
=£12

£10
+£5
+£1
+£1
+ 50 p
+ 20 p
+ 10 p
+ 10 p
+ 10 p
= £18

1 ✎ **Write.**

	wish	How much is it?	money 🐷	yes	no
Tim	racing car	£ 18	£ 20	✔	
Emily	c _ _ _ _ _ _	£	£		
Susan	d _ _ _ _	£	£		

2 💬 Say: Tim wants to have the racing car. It's 18 pounds. He has got 20 pounds.

Emily wants to have … It's … She has got …

3 ✎ **What do you want to have? Write.**

I want to have _____

_____

4 ✎ **Fill in your portfolio.**

Sally 3 Activity Book Förderheft (Englisch ab Klasse 1) © 2017 Cornelsen Verlag GmbH, Berlin

Sally in the snow

1 ✏️ **Read, write and number.**

(6) Sally puts on her **scarf**.

(8) Sally puts on her **gloves**.

(2) Sally puts on her **trousers**.

( ) Sally puts on her **woolly hat**.

( ) Sally puts on her **boots**.

( ) Sally puts on her T-shirt

and her socks.

( ) Sally puts on her pullover.

( ) Sally puts on her jacket.

2 ✏️ **What is Sally wearing? Write.**

Sally is wearing her scarf, her woolly hat,

her gloves, her _____

_____

_____

_____

3 💬 **What are you wearing? Tell.**

I'm wearing ...

Sally 3 Activity Book Förderheft (Englisch ab Klasse 1) © 2017 Cornelsen Verlag GmbH, Berlin

My clothes

1 ✎ **Match the pictures and the words. Write.**

a pair of trousers   T-shirt   jacket   pullover

a pair of jeans

dress

coat

a pair of shorts

shirt

cap ●

shoes

skirt

gloves   socks   scarf   woolly hat   boots

2 ✎ **Winter or summer holidays? Pack your suitcase and write.**

For my summer holidays, I pack

a T-shirt, a pair of shorts,

a pair of jeans, a cap, shoes,

socks.

Girls: a skirt, a dress

For my winter holidays, I pack

_____

_____

_____

_____

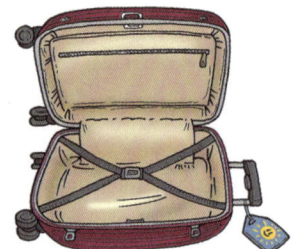

3 ✎ **Fill in your portfolio.**

Sally 3 Activity Book Förderheft (Englisch ab Klasse 1) © 2017 Cornelsen Verlag GmbH, Berlin

When can we meet?

1  **When can the children meet? Listen and draw lines.**

Hi. Let's meet on _____.

Susan

Monday
Friday
Saturday
Wednesday
Tuesday
Thursday
Sunday

2 ✏️ **Write the days in the correct order.**

1 _____
2 Tuesday
3 _____

4 Thursday
5 _____
6 Saturday

7 _____

3 👧👦 **Work in groups. Find out when you can meet.**

name	Mon	Tue	Wed	Thu	Fri	Sat	Sun

Can we meet on Monday/...?

Yes, we can. ✔

○ We can meet on _____.

No, we can't. —

○ We can't meet.

Sally 3 Activity Book Förderheft (Englisch ab Klasse 1) © 2017 Cornelsen Verlag GmbH, Berlin

The wind and the sun

1 🔘 **Listen.**

2 ✂️ ✏️ **Cut out the speech bubbles (page 47), match and stick in.**

I'm stronger than you.

I can make the man take off his coat. I'm the strongest.

3 👦👧 **Read the speech bubbles with your partner.**

4 ✏️ **Write.**

strong

stronger

strongest

strong
stronger
strongest

CD 1.33

Sally 3 Activity Book Förderheft (Englisch ab Klasse 1) © 2017 Cornelsen Verlag GmbH, Berlin

What's the weather like?

1 **Listen and write the weather words.**

Hi there. This is **Tim** from London with the weather forecast. It's another foggy and _____ day. So stay at home.

Good morning from Rome. This is **Emily** with the weather forecast. It's _____ and sunny . Don't forget your suncream.

Hi, this is **Susan** with the weather forecast from Istanbul. Today it's _____ and very windy . Hold on to your hats.

Good morning, this is **Eric** from Berlin. Here's the weather forecast. It's cloudy and snowy . Put on your boots.

cloudy   cold   foggy   hot   rainy   snowy   sunny   windy

2 🐨 **Make your own weather forecast. Write and draw.**

Hello. This is _____

from _____

Today it's _____ and _____ .

3 ✏ **Fill in your portfolio.**

Sally 3 Activity Book Förderheft (Englisch ab Klasse 1) © 2017 Cornelsen Verlag GmbH, Berlin

Happy birthday

1 ✏️ **Read and write.**

card

cake

present

crown

candle

balloon

party

birthday

2 ✏️ **Look in your Pupil's Book on page 23.**
Write your own birthday invitation.

Birthday invitation

Dear _____ ,

Please come to my birthday party.

When: _____

_____

Where: _____

_____

Yours, _____

3 ✏️ **How old are you?** I'm _____ .

When's your birthday? My birthday is in _____ .

Sally 3 Activity Book Förderheft (Englisch ab Klasse 1) © 2017 Cornelsen Verlag GmbH, Berlin

Seasons and months

1 ✎ **Read and write.**

2 ✎ **Write the correct months under each picture.**

In winter

I like the ❄ snow and ice

and Christmas Day. All this is nice.

December, January,

February

In _____ I like the flowers,

 Easter eggs

and April showers.

March, April, May

In _____ I like Halloween,

the 👻 ghosts

and witches I have seen.

September, October,

November

In _____

I like the ☀ sun,

the holidays and lots of fun!

June, July, August

| summer   spring   winter   autumn |

3 ✎ **Fill in your portfolio.**

Sally 3 Activity Book Förderheft (Englisch ab Klasse 1) © 2017 Cornelsen Verlag GmbH, Berlin

Best friends

1  Listen and draw lines.

Susan

Tim

Emily

Eric

Phil

Liz

2 Look and write.

Susan's best friend is _____ .

Tim's best friend is _____ .

Emily's _____ .

And who is your best friend? My _____ .

Who is it?

He has got short brown hair.
He is wearing a grey cap.

She has got long blond hair.
She is wearing a green pullover.

3 Describe your friend. Write. Talk to your partner.

He/She is a _____ . He/She is _____ years old.

He/She has got _____ hair and _____ eyes.

He/She is wearing a _____

_____ .

girl boy blond black red brown
blue pink purple white green
yellow grey pullover shirt T-shirt

he   she

 Can you describe other people?

Sally 3 Activity Book Förderheft (Englisch ab Klasse 1) © 2017 Cornelsen Verlag GmbH, Berlin

My family

1 ✎ **Find the words.**

mother mum grandfather brother aunt sister father uncle grandma grandpa

2 ✎ **Do the crossword.**

| 1 b r o t h e r | 4 f a t h e r |

3 → ← 1
← 2
6 →
3

3 💿 ✎ **Listen and point. Fill in the missing words.**

I've got a mother,

a father and a brother.

I've got a _____ and two brothers .

I haven't got a father or a sister .

I've got a mother and a _____

and a sister .

I've got a mother and a father

and a _____ and a _____ .

💬 **And you? Have you got brothers or sisters?**

Sally 3 Activity Book Förderheft (Englisch ab Klasse 1) © 2017 Cornelsen Verlag GmbH, Berlin

My family tree

1 ✏️✏️ **Draw your family. Fill in the names.**

grandma   grandpa   grandma   grandpa

mum   dad

sister(s)   me   brother(s)

2 ✏️ **Write.**

I've got _____

_____

3 💬 **Present your family to your class.**

4 ✏️ **Fill in your portfolio.**

Sally 3 Activity Book Förderheft (Englisch ab Klasse 1) © 2017 Cornelsen Verlag GmbH, Berlin

My favourite drink

1 ✏️ **What can you see in the mirror? Write.**

coffee

orange juice   milk

lemonade

water   tea   ~~milk~~   coke   hot chocolate   ~~coffee~~   ~~orange juice~~   ~~lemonade~~

2 ✏️ **Hot drink or cold drink? Make a list.**

hot	cold
coffee,	coke,

3 ✏️ **Read and answer.**

What drinks do you like?   🙂   I like _____

What drink do you like best?   🙂🙂   I like _____ best.

What drinks don't you like?   ☹️   I don't like _____

4 ✏️ **Fill in your portfolio.**

Sally 3 Activity Book Förderheft (Englisch ab Klasse 1) © 2017 Cornelsen Verlag GmbH, Berlin

Food and drinks for breakfast

1 ✎ Draw lines.

ham   cheese   tea   honey   coffee

milk   toast   jam   bread   orange juice

butter   water   roll   egg   cornflakes

2 ✎ Find the words.

honeyrolljam
coffeeteacheese
buttermilkeggwater
breadtoastrollham
cornflakeseggbreadtea

3 ✎ Food or drink? Fill in.

food

drinks

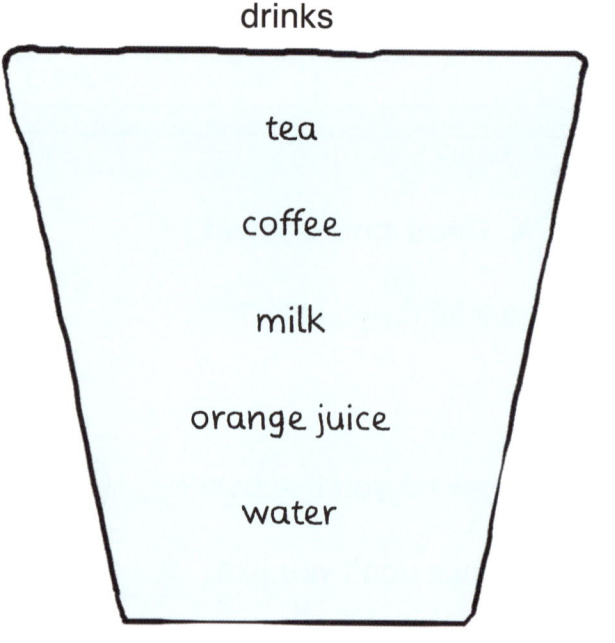

tea

coffee

milk

orange juice

water

 Do you know more food or drink words? Tell your partner.

Sally 3 Activity Book Förderheft (Englisch ab Klasse 1) © 2017 Cornelsen Verlag GmbH, Berlin

What do you have for breakfast?

1 ✎ **Look at the children. What do they have for breakfast?**

Eric has cornflakes and _____ .

Emily has hot chocolate and _____

_____ and _____ .

Liz has a roll , _____ and _____ .

2 ✎✎ **Fill your plate, your glass and your cup.**

● For breakfast, I have

_____ and

_____ and

_____ .

3 ✎ **What do the children say?**

   I have   Can   the      please?

Can I have the milk , please?

   the   I have   Can   please?

Can I have _____

please?   the   🧈   I have   Can

_____

Can   please?   the   🍯   I have

_____

4 ✎ **Fill in your portfolio.**

Sally 3 Activity Book Förderheft (Englisch ab Klasse 1) © 2017 Cornelsen Verlag GmbH, Berlin

Fruit mix

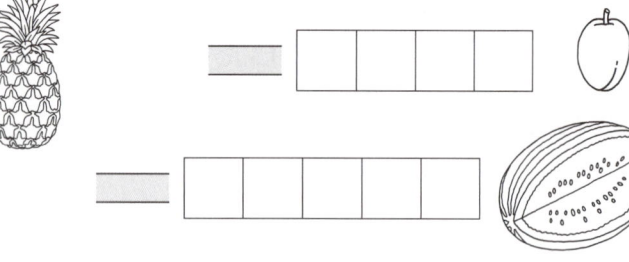

melon ~~cherry~~ ~~pineapple~~ strawberry
plum orange banana apple

1 ✏️✏️ **Write and colour.**

a | p | i | n | e | a | p | p | l | e |

a | c | h | e | r | r | y |

an | | | | | |

| | | | | | |

What's missing?
Draw the fruit and write.

It's a _____ .

a **ch**erry – a **b**anana
an **a**pple – an **o**range

2 💿 **Listen and number.**

3 💿✏️ **Listen and tick ✔: yes or no?**

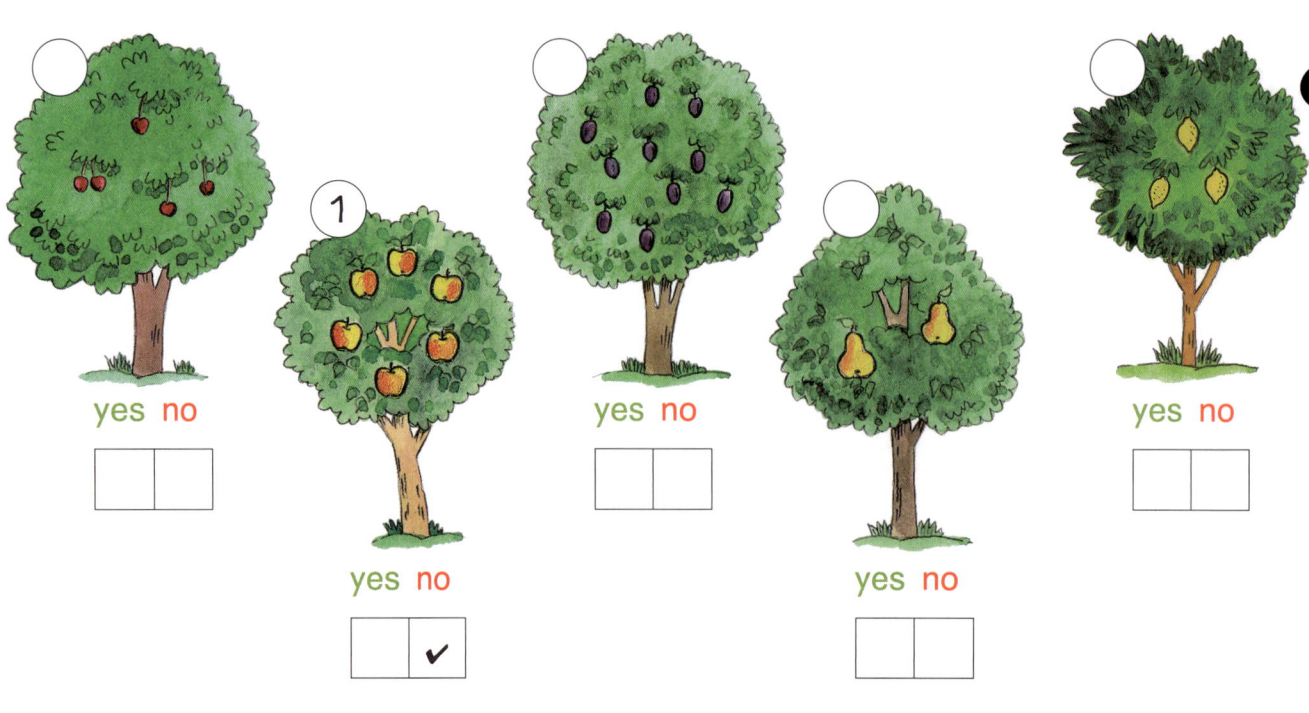

yes no

1

yes no

yes no

yes no ✔

yes no

yes no

Sally 3 Activity Book Förderheft (Englisch ab Klasse 1) © 2017 Cornelsen Verlag GmbH, Berlin

At the ice cream stand

1 🔘 ✏️ What does Emily buy? Listen and tick ✔.
What does Phil buy? Listen and tick ✔.

2 ✏️ Fill in the speech bubbles. Act out the dialogue.

Hello.

_____.
Can I help you?

Yes. I'd like
two scoops, please,
_____
and _____.

Here you are. That's
£ _____, please.

Here you are.

Thank you. Goodbye.

_____.

3 ✏️ ✏️ What would you like? Write and colour.

I'd like _____.

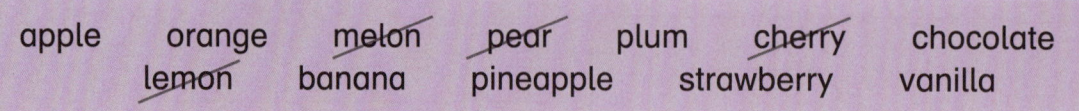

Ice cream rock

1 💿 ✏️ **Listen to the song. Look and write.**

I scream,   you scream,   we   scream   for   ice cream. You

scream,   they scream,   we   scream   for   ice   cream.

One   scoop   of   or- ange,   one scoop of   plum,

one scoop of cher- ry,   one scoop   of   le- mon.

One scoop of  🍊 _____, one scoop of 🫐 _____,

one scoop of 🍒 cherry ,   one scoop of 🍋 lemon .

One scoop of 🍑 _____,   one scoop of 🍐 pear ,

one scoop of 🍫 _____,   one scoop of 🍈 melon .

| apple | orange | ~~melon~~ | ~~pear~~ | plum | ~~cherry~~ | chocolate |
| lemon | banana | pineapple | strawberry | vanilla |

2 ✏️ **Now it's your turn. Write.**

One scoop of _____, one scoop of _____

_____ .

3 ✏️ **Fill in your portfolio.**

Sally 3 Activity Book Förderheft (Englisch ab Klasse 1) © 2017 Cornelsen Verlag GmbH, Berlin

Our pets

1 ✏️ **Do the crossword.**

budgie   cat   dog
fish   ~~guinea pig~~
hamster   mouse
rabbit

2 ✏️ **What's your favourite pet?**

My favourite pet is a

_____ .

Its name is

_____ .

It is _____ .

It is _____ .

black   brown   grey
white   big   small …

3 ✏️ **Draw your favourite pet.**

⭐ **Find more pets in your dictionary.**
Describe them to your partner.

Sally 3 Activity Book Förderheft (Englisch ab Klasse 1) © 2017 Cornelsen Verlag GmbH, Berlin

Pets

Little dog lost

1 Listen.

   **2** Cut out the speech bubbles (page 47), match and stick in.

Lost pets

1 ✏️ **Read and number.**

cat **1**
grey and white
green eyes

rabbit **2**
white, red eyes, eats carrots
We miss Roger very much!

● | tortoise **3** |
| --- |
| green and brown, |
| eats lettuce |
| small head |

two guinea pigs **4**
brown and white

hamster **5**
brown and yellow

● | budgie **6** |
| --- |
| blue with a yellow head |

three mice **7**
small
grey, white and black

1 dog – 2 dogs
1 cat – 2 cats

1 mouse – 2 mice
1 fish – 2 fish

2 ✏️ **Read and colour.**

3 ✏️ **What's missing? Draw the pets.**

4 ✏️ **Fill in your portfolio.**

Sally 3 Activity Book Förderheft (Englisch ab Klasse 1) © 2017 Cornelsen Verlag GmbH, Berlin

100 little kangaroos are sitting on Big Ben

1 ✂️✏️ Cut out the puzzle (page 49).
Match the numbers and stick in.

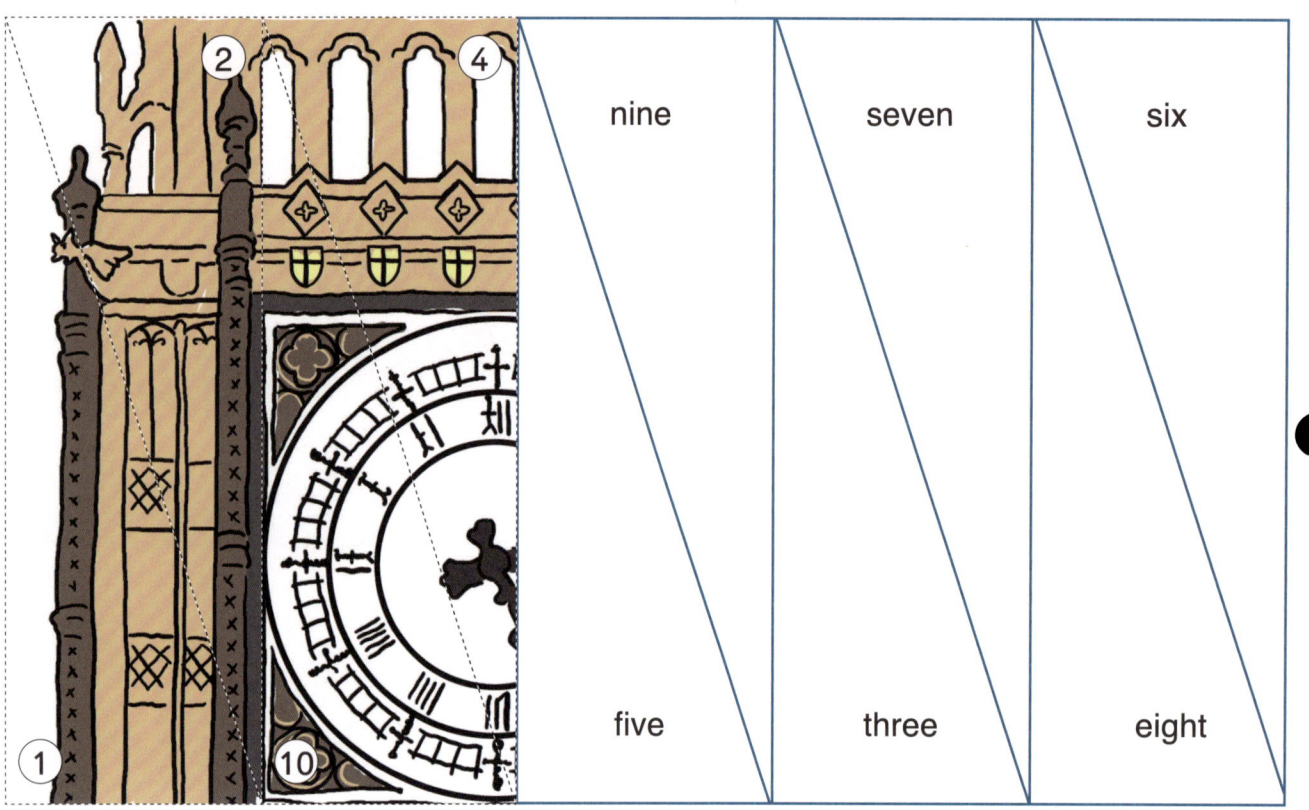

nine   seven   six

five   three   eight

2 🖍️ Listen and colour.

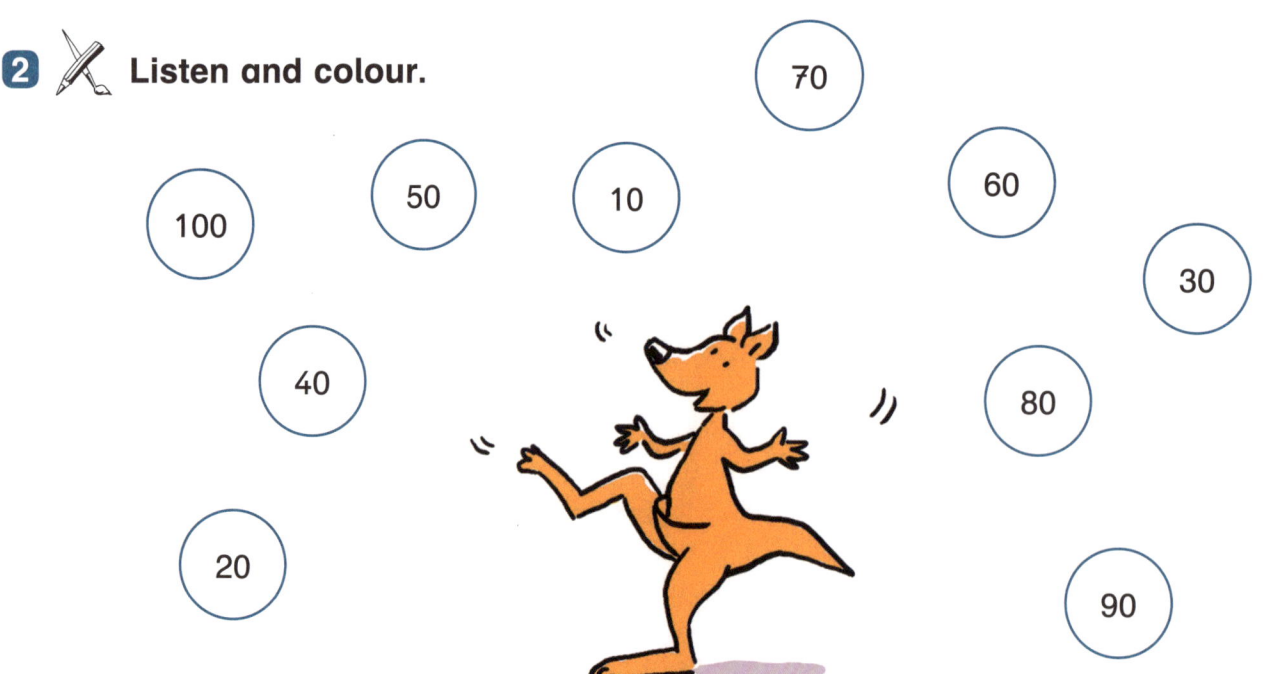

70

50   10

100   60

30

40   80

20   90

⭐ Count backwards from 20 to 1.

Sally 3 Activity Book Förderheft (Englisch ab Klasse 1) © 2017 Cornelsen Verlag GmbH, Berlin

At Madame Tussaud's

1 Listen and number.

2 Tick ✔ the correct answer.

3 What do you want to see in London?

I want to see _____ .

The tickets are	£60.	✔
	£18.	
	£20.	
Susan loves	Prince William.	
	Kate's dress.	
	Prince Harry.	
Tim wants to see	Schwarzenegger.	
	Mozart.	
	Johnny Depp.	

I want to see Big Ben.

Sally 3 Activity Book Förderheft (Englisch ab Klasse 1) © 2017 Cornelsen Verlag GmbH, Berlin

Farm animals

On the farm

1 ✏️ **Look and write.**

duck   hen   goose   sheep   pig   cow   horse

in   on   under   in front of   next to   behind

The pig is in the barn.

The _____ is in front of the house.

The _____ is next to the chair.

The _____ is behind the tree.

The goose is _____ the roof.

The hen is _____ the table.

The duck is _____ the pond.

2 ✏️ **Fill in your portfolio.**

On the beach

1 ✎ **Trace the lines and write.**

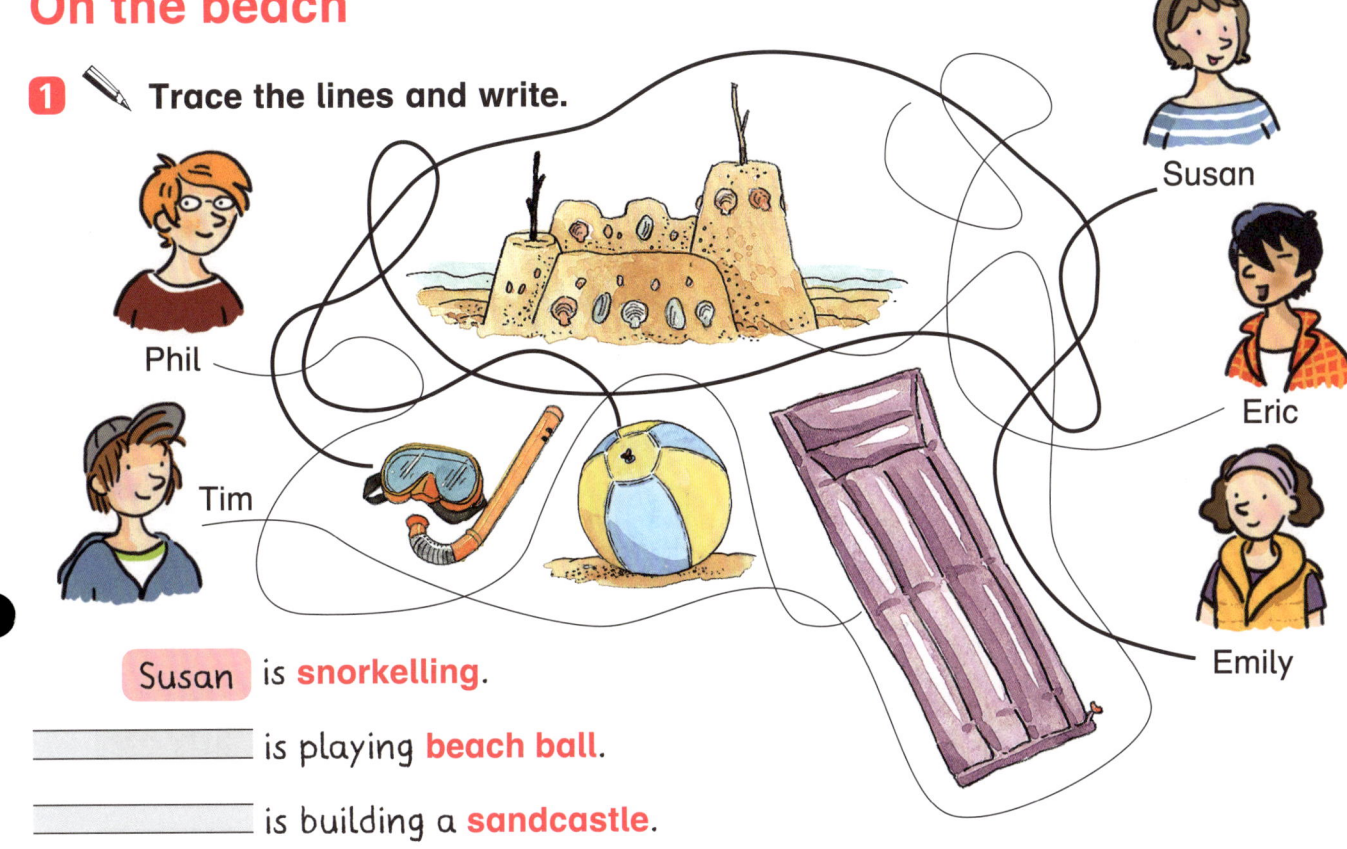

Phil

Tim

Susan

Eric

Emily

Susan is **snorkelling**.

_____ is playing **beach ball**.

_____ is building a **sandcastle**.

_____ is lying on an **airbed**.

_____ is doing **nothing**!

2 ✎ **Find the words.**

sandcastle airbed snorkelling summer beach sun sea

3 ✎ **Odd one out!**

T-shirt
sunglasses
shorts
scarf

ice cream
Easter egg
beach ball
airbed

school
summer
sea
snorkelling

4 ✎ **Fill in your portfolio.**

Sally 3 Activity Book Förderheft (Englisch ab Klasse 1) © 2017 Cornelsen Verlag GmbH, Berlin

Robin Hood's clever trick

1 Listen.

2 Cut out the speech bubbles (page 49), match and stick in.

3 Act out the story.

Sally 3 Activity Book Förderheft (Englisch ab Klasse 1) © 2017 Cornelsen Verlag GmbH, Berlin

It's Halloween

1 🔘 ✏️ **Listen and match.**

2 🔘 ✏️ **Listen and circle ◯ the parts of the body.**

3 🔘 ✏️ **Find Emily's costume. Listen and tick ✔.**

▢   ▢

4 ✏️ 🧑‍🤝‍🧑 **Draw your own Halloween costume and tell your partner.**

> Trick or treat,
> trick or treat!
> Give me something
> sweet to eat.

On Halloween,

I'm a _____.

Sally 3 Activity Book Förderheft (Englisch ab Klasse 1) © 2017 Cornelsen Verlag GmbH, Berlin

A chubby little snowman

A chubby little
has a carrot
along jumps
and what do you suppose?

That hungry little kangaroo,
looking for her lunch,
eats the snowman's nose,
nibble, nibble, CRUNCH!

1 Listen.

2 Cut out the rhyme (page 51), find the correct order and stick in.

3 Draw pictures.

4 Learn the rhyme.

Sally 3 Activity Book Förderheft (Englisch ab Klasse 1) © 2017 Cornelsen Verlag GmbH, Berlin

Christmas Eve

1  **Listen and number.**

( ) stocking (3) presents (5) Christmas cards

(1) bed ( ) reindeer ( ) Father Christmas

2 **Draw lines.**

Christmas tree   chimney   sleigh   present

reindeer   Father Christmas   stocking

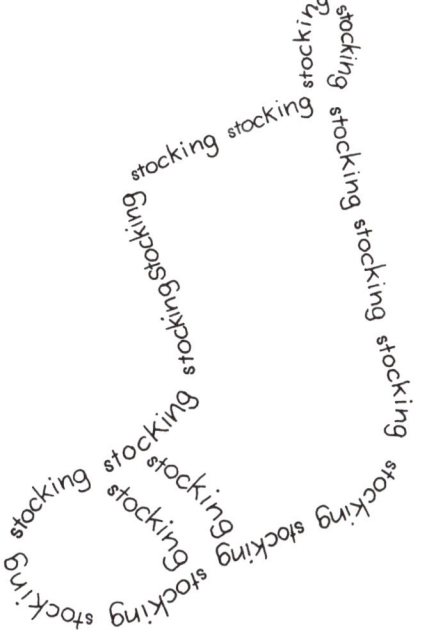

3 **Now it's your turn!**

_ _ _ _ _ _ _ Christmas Christmas Christmas

_ _ _ _ _ _ _

_ _ _ _ _ _ tree tree

_ _ _ _ _ _ tree tree

tree tree tree tree

Sally 3 Activity Book Förderheft (Englisch ab Klasse 1) © 2017 Cornelsen Verlag GmbH, Berlin

Edgar's Easter eggs

1 🔊 ✏️ **Listen and number.**

 happy [ ]
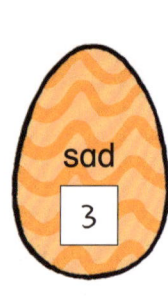 sad [3]
 Easter eggs [1]
 basket [ ]
 colour [2]
 share [ ]

2 ✂️ 📎 **Cut out the speech bubbles (page 51), match and stick in.**

Where are the Easter eggs?

1 🖊 **Hide your eggs. Fill in the words.**

The blue egg is ⬚ in front of ⬚ the bush.

The red egg is ⬚ behind ⬚ the fence.

The brown egg is ⬚ next to ⬚ the flower.

The yellow egg is ⬚⬚⬚⬚⬚⬚ the tree.

The pink egg is ⬚⬚⬚⬚⬚⬚ the basket.

⚫ The purple egg is ⬚⬚⬚⬚⬚⬚ Edgar.

The green egg is ⬚⬚⬚⬚⬚⬚ Edgar's mother.

> in
> on
> under
> next to
> in front of
> behind

2 ✏ **Draw and colour the Easter eggs.**

3 👦👧 **Find your partner's Easter eggs.**

> Is the blue egg under the bush?

> Yes, it is.

> No, it isn't.

Let's talk

1 ✂️✏️ Cut out the speech bubbles ♡ (page 51). Match and stick in.

2 ✎ Write more dialogues.

3 👦👧 Act out the dialogues with a partner.

Sally 3 Activity Book Förderheft (Englisch ab Klasse 1) © 2017 Cornelsen Verlag GmbH, Berlin

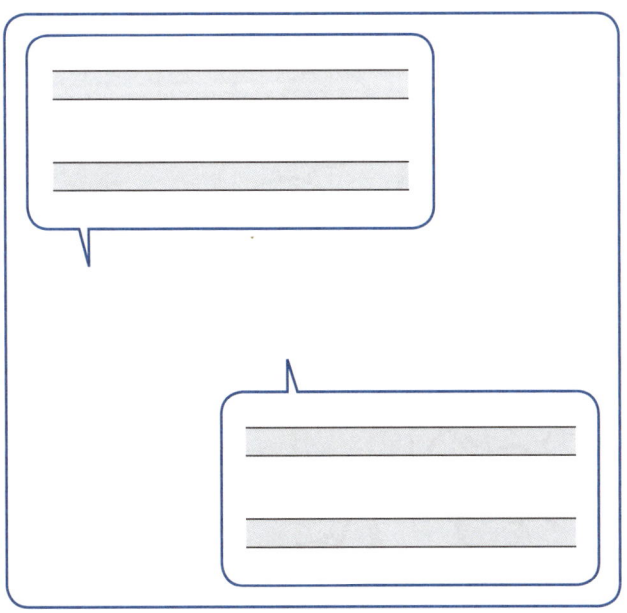

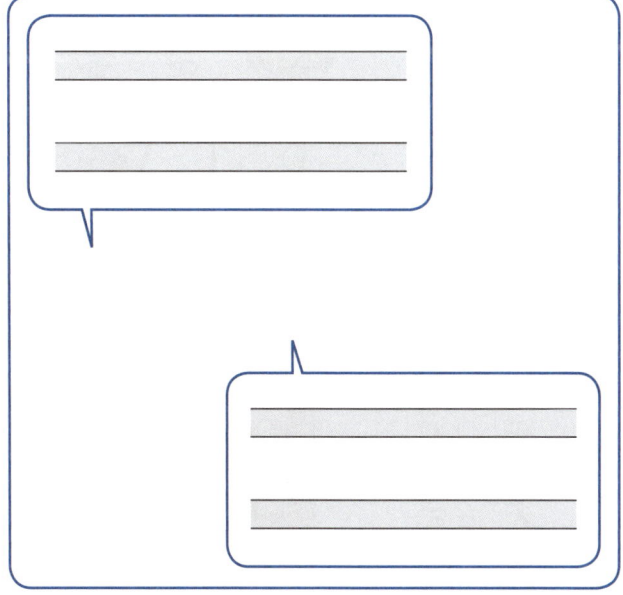

Sally 3 Activity Book Förderheft (Englisch ab Klasse 1) © 2017 Cornelsen Verlag GmbH, Berlin

Board game

1 ✏ Fill in the speech bubbles.

2 Play the game with your friends.

🎲 Roll the dice. Take turns.

💬 If you land on a speech bubble, answer the question.

🐕 Move one field forward.

🐕 Move one field backward.

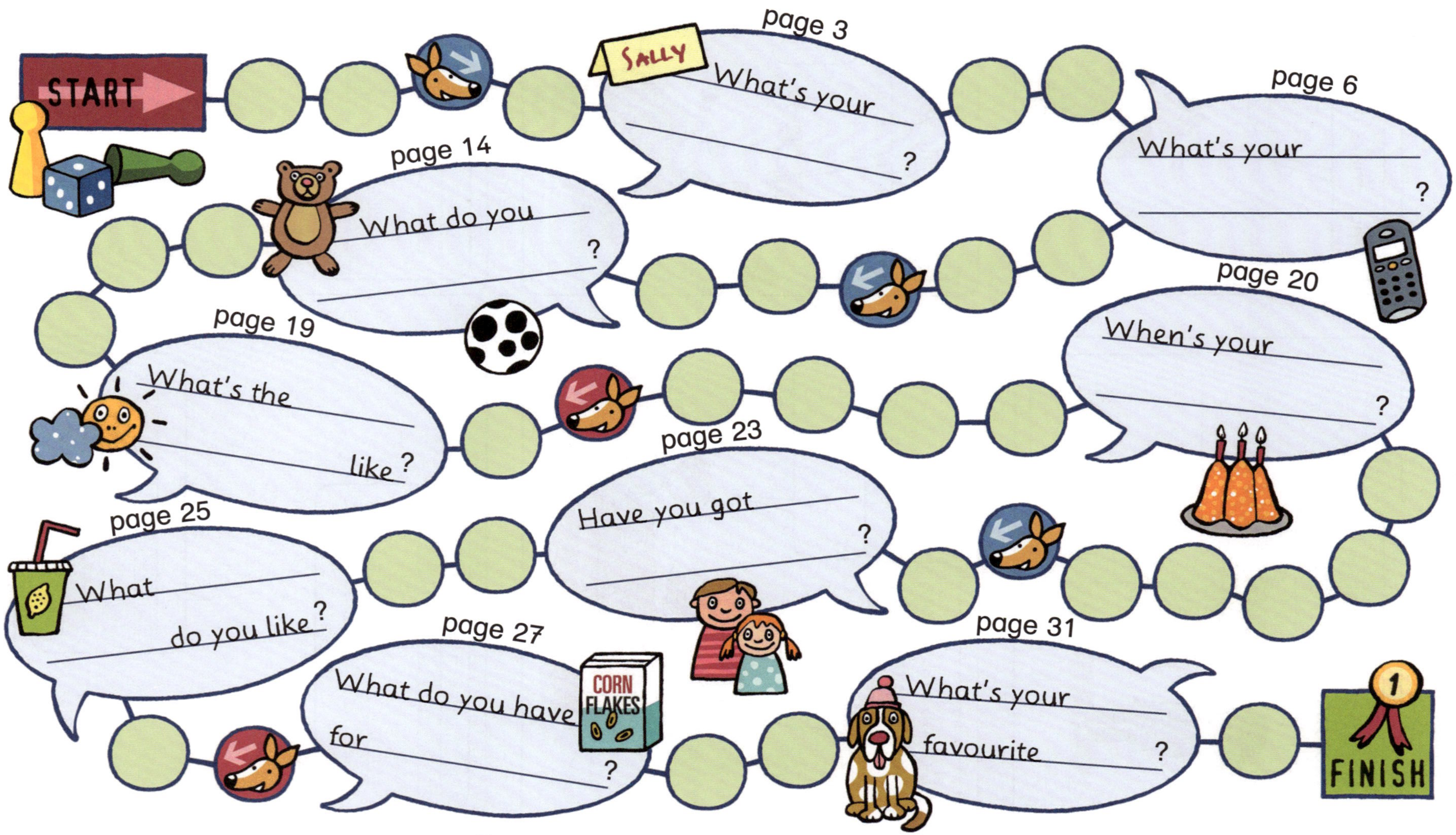

START

FINISH 🥇

Page 6 — What's your _____ ?

page 20 — When's your _____ ?

Page 3 — What's your _____ ?

SALLY

page 14 — What do you _____ ?

page 23 — Have you got _____ ?

page 31 — What's your favourite _____ ?

page 19 — What's the _____ like ?

page 27 — What do you have for _____ ?

page 25 — What _____ do you like ?

Sally 3 Activity Book Förderheft (Englisch ab Klasse 1) © 2017 Cornelsen Verlag GmbH, Berlin

✂ Get up, Susan! (page 10)

✂ The wind and the sun (page 18)

No, I'm stronger than you.	See, I'm stronger than you. I'm the strongest!
	You can never do this. I can make the man take off his coat. I'm the strongest.

✂ Little dog lost (page 32)

Thank you very much.	Mummy, where is Bobby?
Hello. Can I help you?	

✁ 100 little kangaroos are sitting on Big Ben (page 34)

✁ Robin Hood's clever trick (page 38)

| Thank you, Robin Hood! | Where's my hat? | Help! Help! | Hands up! |

A chubby little snowman (page 40)

The snowman turns

from to (😟)

and Sally knows that this is bad.

Off she jumps

and hop, hop, hop,

she goes to get a  .

Edgar's Easter eggs (page 42)

Beautiful eggs!

Thank you, Edgar.
You're my best friend.

Let's colour
Easter eggs.

No!

Let's talk (page 44, 45)

My name is Jenny.

I'm 9 years old.

What's your
telephone number?

When is your
birthday?

No, thank you.

I like water and
tea.

Yes, I've got
a sister and
a brother

Sally

Mein Sprachenportfolio
Klasse 3

My name is _____.

**So habe ich
im Englischunterricht gearbeitet:**

	1. Halbjahr	2. Halbjahr
Ich habe aufmerksam zugehört.	🟢🟡🔴	🟢🟡🔴
Ich habe mich regelmäßig gemeldet.	🟢🟡🔴	🟢🟡🔴
Ich habe versucht, neue Wörter genau nachzusprechen.	🟢🟡🔴	🟢🟡🔴
Ich habe versucht, in Gesprächen möglichst viel auf Englisch zu sagen.	🟢🟡🔴	🟢🟡🔴
Ich habe die Lieder mitgesungen.	🟢🟡🔴	🟢🟡🔴
Ich habe mindestens einen Reim gründlich geübt und aufgesagt.	🟢🟡🔴	🟢🟡🔴
Ich habe bei den Hörübungen genau zugehört.	🟢🟡🔴	🟢🟡🔴
Ich konnte verstehen, was meine Lehrerin / mein Lehrer auf Englisch sagt.	🟢🟡🔴	🟢🟡🔴
Ich habe Wörter richtig abgeschrieben.	🟢🟡🔴	🟢🟡🔴
Ich konnte schon kleine Texte schreiben.	🟢🟡🔴	🟢🟡🔴

Sally 3 Activity Book Förderheft (Englisch ab Klasse 1) © 2017 Cornelsen Verlag GmbH, Berlin

Name: ════════════════════

Geburtstag: ══════════════

Geburtsort: ══════════════

Geburtsland: ═════════════

═════════════════════════

Diese Sprachen kann ich sprechen:

═════════════════════════════════

Diese Sprachen kann ich verstehen:

═════════════════════════════════

Diese Sprachen lerne ich in der Schule:

═════════════════════════════════

═════════════════════════════════

Diese Sprachen möchte ich gerne noch lernen:

═════════════════════════════════

In diesen Ländern, in denen andere Sprachen gesprochen werden,
war ich schon einmal:

═════════════════════════════════

═════════════════════════════════

So habe ich mich dort verständigt:

═════════════════════════════════

═════════════════════════════════

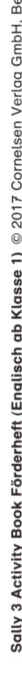

Sally 3 Activity Book Förderheft (Englisch ab Klasse 1) © 2017 Cornelsen Verlag GmbH, Berlin

three **3**

1 ✏ **Diese Wörter kenne ich schon auf Englisch:**

2 ✏ **Ich kenne auch Wörter aus anderen Sprachen:**

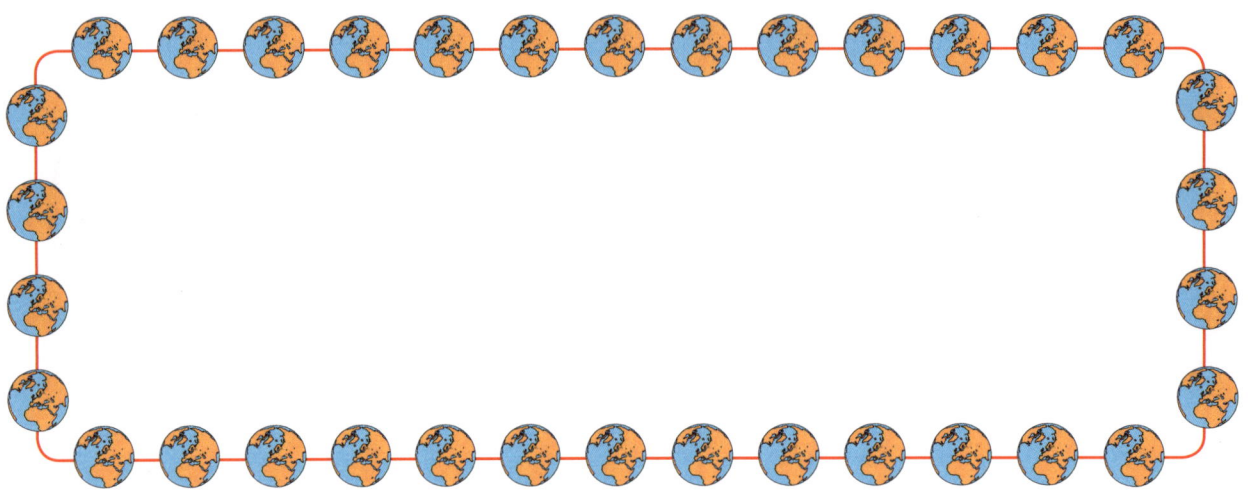

3 **Ich kann mich vorstellen und sagen, was ich mag:**

Hello, my name is _____ .

I like _____ .

4 **Das kann ich auch schon auf Englisch:**

Ich kann sagen, wie es mir geht.

Ich kann andere fragen, wie es ihnen geht.

Sally 3 Activity Book Förderheft (Englisch ab Klasse 1) © 2017 Cornelsen Verlag GmbH, Berlin

1  **Diese Farben kann ich benennen und aufschreiben:**

Male die Kleckse in verschiedenen Farben aus.
Hilfe findest du im Activity Book auf Seite 5.

_____ _____ _____ _____

_____ _____ _____ _____

green   red   yellow   blue   pink   brown   black   white

2 **So habe ich „Sally's rhyme" geübt:**

_____

_____

3 **Ich kann meine Telefonnummer auf Englisch nennen:**

What's your telephone number?

My telephone number is _____ .

4 **Das kann ich auch schon auf Englisch:**

Ich kann andere nach ihrer Telefonnummer fragen.

Ich kann die Nummer verstehen und aufschreiben.

Ich kann von 1 bis 10 zählen.

Ich kann rückwärts von 10 bis 1 zählen.

Sally 3 Activity Book Förderheft (Englisch ab Klasse 1) © 2017 Cornelsen Verlag GmbH, Berlin

1 ✎ **Ich kann aufschreiben, was in meiner Schultasche ist:**

Hilfe findest du im Activity Book auf Seite 7.

2 **Ich kann die Wörter in, on und under verwenden, um zu sagen, wo etwas ist:** ✔

 ☐ under

 ☐ on

 ☐ in

3 **Ich kann auf Englisch etwas über meinen Schultag erzählen und aufschreiben (in welche Schule ich gehe usw.):**

I go to _____

I'm in class _____

My teacher is _____

_____

Sally 3 Activity Book Förderheft (Englisch ab Klasse 1) © 2017 Cornelsen Verlag GmbH, Berlin

3 **Das kann ich auch schon auf Englisch:**

Ich kann das Lied „Head and shoulders" singen.

○ ○ ○

Ich kann den Comic „Ouch!" verstehen und vorspielen.

○ ○ ○

Ich kann die Geschichte „Get up, Susan!" verstehen
und die Bewegungen machen.

○ ○ ○

Ich kann sagen, wie ich mich fühle und auch warum.

○ ○ ○

Ich kann das Lied „If you're happy" singen.

○ ○ ○

4 ✎ **Ich habe eine eigene Strophe zum Lied „If you're happy"
erfunden und vorgetragen. Das ist meine Strophe:**

If you're _____ and you know it, _____

_____

_____

5 **Feedback**

Das hat mir in dieser Unit am meisten Spaß gemacht:

_____

_____

Das hat mir nicht gefallen:

_____

_____

Sally 3 Activity Book Förderheft (Englisch ab Klasse 1) © 2017 Cornelsen Verlag GmbH, Berlin

 **Ich kann diese Spielzeuge benennen: ✔**

Hilfe findest du im Activity Book auf den Seiten 13 und 14.

☐   ☐   ☐

☐   ☐   ☐

Ich kenne auch noch diese Spielzeuge:

2 The fish who could wish

Das hat mir geholfen, die Geschichte zu verstehen: ✔

☐ Ich habe mir vorgestellt, was in der Geschichte passiert.

☐ Ich habe beim Hören auf Wörter geachtet, die ich schon kenne.

☐ Ich habe mir die Bilder im Pupil's Book angesehen.

☐ Ich habe den Text im Pupil's Book mitgelesen.

Sally 3 Activity Book Förderheft (Englisch ab Klasse 1) © 2017 Cornelsen Verlag GmbH, Berlin

3 Numbers

Ich kann auf Englisch bis 20 zählen.

Ich kann auch in Zehnerschritten weiterzählen (30, 40, …).

4 Ich kann fragen und sagen, wie viel etwas kostet:

Hilfe findest du im Pupil's Book auf Seite 15.

How much is the ?

It's _____ pounds.

5 Feedback

Das hat mir in dieser Unit am meisten Spaß gemacht:

_____

_____

_____

_____

Das hat mir nicht gefallen:

_____

_____

_____

_____

Sally 3 Activity Book Förderheft (Englisch ab Klasse 1) © 2017 Cornelsen Verlag GmbH, Berlin

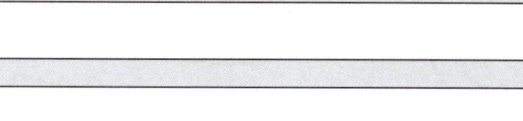

1 ✏️ **Ich kann diese Kleidungsstücke benennen ✔ und aufschreiben:**

Hilfe findest du im Activity Book auf den Seiten 15 und 16.

☐ _____ ☐ _____ ☐ _____ ☐ _____

☐ _____ ☐ _____ ☐ _____

cap   gloves   shoes   skirt   pullover   T-shirt   socks

2 **Sally in the snow**

Ich kann die Geschichte „Sally in the snow" verstehen.

Ich kann die Sätze den Bildern zuordnen:

Sally puts on her pullover.

Sally puts on her trousers.

Sally is wearing her scarf, her jacket and her gloves.

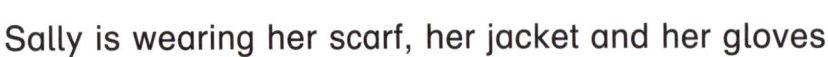

Sally 3 Activity Book Förderheft (Englisch ab Klasse 1) © 2017 Cornelsen Verlag GmbH, Berlin

3 💬✏️ **Ich kann sagen und aufschreiben, was ich heute anhabe:**

I'm wearing my _____

_____

jeans   T-shirt   pullover

4 **So merke ich mir neue Wörter:** ✔

☐ Ich stelle mir ein Bild dazu vor.

☐ Ich schreibe mir das Wort auf.

☐ Ich spreche mir das Wort ganz oft vor.

☐ Ich merke mir Sätze, in denen das Wort vorkommt.

5 **That's what I can do**

Hier ist Platz für deine Ideen. Du kannst ein Rätsel erfinden, etwas zum Thema „clothes"
schreiben oder malen, Bilder aus einem Katalog ausschneiden und beschriften usw.

Sally 3 Activity Book Förderheft (Englisch ab Klasse 1) © 2017 Cornelsen Verlag GmbH, Berlin

1 ✏️ **Ich kann die Wochentage in der richtigen Reihenfolge abschreiben:** Hilfe findest du im Activity Book auf Seite 17.

_____

_____

Monday Sunday Tuesday Friday Wednesday Thursday Saturday

2 ✏️ **Ich kann mich mit jemandem verabreden:**

Can we meet on _____ ?

No, sorry. I can't.

And on _____ ?

Yes, great. Let's meet on _____ .

3 💬 **Ich kann sagen, wie das Wetter ist:** ✔

☐ 🎏 In London it's windy.

☐ ☁️ In Berlin it's cloudy.

☐ ☀️ In Istanbul it's sunny.

☐ 🌧️ In Rome it's rainy.

4 **Das kann ich auch schon auf Englisch:**

Ich kann eine eigene Wettervorhersage schreiben.

Ich kann die Wettervorhersage vortragen.

Beim Vortragen achte ich auf diese Dinge besonders: ✔

☐ Ich spreche laut und deutlich.

☐ Ich schaue die Zuhörer an.

☐ Ich zeige Bilder.

Sally 3 Activity Book Förderheft (Englisch ab Klasse 1) © 2017 Cornelsen Verlag GmbH, Berlin

1 ✎ **Ich kann diese Geburtstagswörter benennen:** ✔

Hilfe findest du im Activity Book auf Seite 20.

☐　　　☐　　　☐　　　☐

2 ✎ **Ich kann die Monatsnamen in der richtigen Reihenfolge abschreiben:** Hilfe findest du im Activity Book auf Seite 21.

_____

_____

_____

January　April　March　February　August　June　September
May　July　December　November　October

3 ✎ **Das kann ich auch schon auf Englisch:**

Ich kann jemanden fragen, wann er Geburtstag hat.

When's your _____?

Ich kann sagen, wann mein Geburtstag ist.

My birthday is in _____.

Ich kann jemandem zum Geburtstag gratulieren.

_____!

Ich kann eine Geburtstagseinladung schreiben.　

Ich kann den Reim „Seasons" verstehen und mitsprechen.　

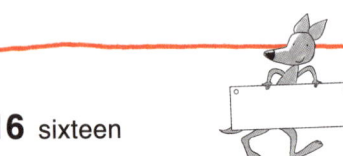
1 ✏️ **Ich kenne die Wörter für die Personen einer Familie:**

Hilfe findest du im Activity Book auf den Seiten 23 und 24
und im Pupil's Book auf Seite 26.

grandmother and grandfather

_____

_____

_____

brother and sister   mother and father

2 ✏️ **Ich kann eine Person (zum Beispiel einen Freund) beschreiben:**

My friend is a _____

He/She is _____ years old.

He/She has got _____ hair and _____ eyes.

He/She is wearing a _____

3 **Das kann ich auch schon auf Englisch:**

Ich kann andere zu ihrer Familie befragen.

Ich kann sagen, wer zu meiner Familie gehört.

Sally 3 Activity Book Förderheft (Englisch ab Klasse 1) © 2017 Cornelsen Verlag GmbH, Berlin

1 ✏️ **Ich kann sagen, welche Getränke ich mag und welche nicht:**
Hilfe findest du im Activity Book auf Seite 25.

I like _____ .

I don't like _____ .

2 ✏️ **Ich kenne auch noch diese kalten und heißen Getränke:**

Cold drinks: _____

Hot drinks: _____

Breakfast

1 💬✏️ **Ich kann sagen und aufschreiben, was ich gern zum Frühstück esse:** Hilfe findest du im Activity Book auf den Seiten 26 und 27.

For breakfast, I have _____

_____

2 💬✏️ **Ich kann mich beim Frühstück verständigen:**

Can I have the _____ , please?

Here you are.

Thank you.

Sally 3 Activity Book Förderheft (Englisch ab Klasse 1) © 2017 Cornelsen Verlag GmbH, Berlin

 **Fruit**

1 Ich kann sagen und aufschreiben, was in den **Obstkörben ist:** Hilfe findest du im Activity Book auf Seite 28.

5 cherries, 2 _____   4 _____ , 2 pears

1 _____ and 1 melon.   and 1 pineapple.

2 Ich kann ein Eis bestellen:

Hilfe findest du im Activity Book auf Seite 29.

Hello, can I help you?

Yes, I'd like two scoops, please, _____ and _____ .

Here you are. That's £2, please.

_____

3 Ich kann sagen, was mein Lieblingseis ist:

_____

4 Das kann ich auch schon auf Englisch:

Ich kann das Gespräch von Phil und Emily am Eisstand verstehen.

Ich kann den „Ice cream rock" singen.

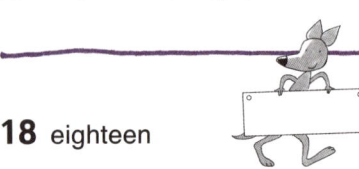

Sally 3 Activity Book Förderheft (Englisch ab Klasse 1) © 2017 Cornelsen Verlag GmbH, Berlin

1 ✎ **Diese Tiere kann ich benennen** ✔ **und aufschreiben:**

Hilfe findest du im Activity Book auf Seite 31.

☐

_____

☐

_____

☐

_____

☐

_____

☐

_____

cat   dog   fish   hamster   mouse

2 ✎ **Ich kann ein Haustier beschreiben.**

My pet is a _____ .

Its name is _____ . It is _____

_____ .

3 **Das kann ich auch schon auf Englisch:**

Ich kann das Lied „Five little pets" singen.

Ich kann die Geschichte „Little dog lost" verstehen.

4 **Feedback**

Das hat mir in dieser Unit am meisten Spaß gemacht:

_____

_____

Das hat mir nicht gefallen:

_____

_____

1 ✏️ **Ich kann Bilder und Wörter zuordnen:**

Hilfe findest du im Activity Book auf Seite 36.

~~1~~	hen
2	horse
3	sheep
4	duck
5	pig
6	goose
7	cow

2 **Das kann ich auch schon auf Englisch:**

Ich kann die Geschichte „Clumsy the dog" verstehen.

Ich kann den „Bingo song" mitsingen.

3 **Animal rally**

Diese Stationen konnte ich gut:

_____

_____

Bei dieser Station brauchte ich Hilfe:

_____

Sally 3 Activity Book Förderheft (Englisch ab Klasse 1) © 2017 Cornelsen Verlag GmbH, Berlin

1 ✏️ **Diese Dinge kann ich auf Englisch benennen:** ✔

Hilfe findest du im Activity Book auf Seite 37.

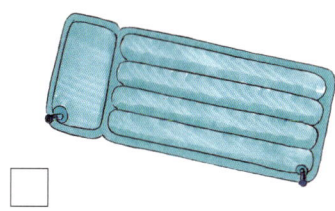

☐   ☐   ☐

2 ✏️ **Ich kann sagen, was die Kinder machen:**

Susan is _____ .

Tim is snorkelling .

Emily is building a _____ .

sandcastle   swimming   ~~snorkelling~~

3 **Das kann ich auch schon auf Englisch:**

Ich kann den Zungenbrecher „She sells seashells" aufsagen.

○ ○ ○

Ich kann das Lied „Hooray, hooray, it's a holi-holiday" singen.

○ ○ ○

Ich habe eine eigene Strophe zum Gedicht „Dreaming of summer" geschrieben und kann sie vortragen.

○ ○ ○

4 **Das hat mir beim Schreiben der Gedichtstrophe geholfen:** ✔

☐ Ich habe vorher Schreibideen gesammelt.

☐ Ich habe Wörter im Wörterbuch nachgeschlagen.

Sally 3 Activity Book Förderheft (Englisch ab Klasse 1) © 2017 Cornelsen Verlag GmbH, Berlin

Hier sammle ich meine Lieblingswörter zu den verschiedenen Themen: Im letzten Feld kannst du eine eigene Überschrift wählen.

Colours and numbers	School
Clothes	Weather
Family and friends	Food and drinks

Sally 3 Activity Book Förderheft (Englisch ab Klasse 1) © 2017 Cornelsen Verlag GmbH, Berlin

Body and feelings	Toys
Seasons and months	Around the year
Animals	

Ich kenne mich gut aus und kann die folgenden Fragen beantworten: ✔

Where's Sally from?		
☐ England	AM	
☐ America	ER	
✔ Australia	EN	

Who brings the Easter eggs?		What do you get for Christmas?	
☐ Father Christmas	LG	☐ reindeer	SI
☐ Easter bunny	GL	☐ chimney	EH
☐ Sally	CA	☐ presents	IS

When is Halloween?		What can you say on Halloween?	
☐ on April 5th	HO	☐ Trick or treat!	SG
☐ on Friday	ME	☐ Spooky nights!	GE
☐ on October 31st	HI	☐ Good luck!	SH

Where does the Queen live?		Who stands in front of Buckingham Palace?	
☐ Loch Ness	OR	☐ the guards	A
☐ Buckingham Palace	RE	☐ Tim and Susan	M
☐ Germany	RA	☐ Madame Tussaud	S

What is not in London?

☐ double-decker bus	☐ London Eye	☐ Statue of Liberty
D	P	T

Trage die Buchstaben der richtigen Lösungen hier der Reihe nach ein.

E	N													!

Sally 3 Activity Book Förderheft (Englisch ab Klasse 1) © 2017 Cornelsen Verlag GmbH, Berlin

4 ✎ **Das weiß ich jetzt über die Schule in England:**

Hilfe findest du im Pupil's Book auf Seite 9.

_____

_____

_____

_____

5 **Das kann ich auch schon auf Englisch:**

Ich kann den „Schoolbag rap" mitsprechen. ○ ○ ○

Ich kann die Geschichte „In the classroom" verstehen. ○ ○ ○

6 **Feedback**

Das hat mir in dieser Unit am meisten Spaß gemacht:

_____

_____

_____

Das hat mir nicht gefallen:

_____

_____

_____

Sally 3 Activity Book Förderheft (Englisch ab Klasse 1) © 2017 Cornelsen Verlag GmbH, Berlin

1  **Diese Körperteile kann ich benennen:** ✔

Hilfe findest du im Activity Book auf den Seiten 9 und 10.

 ☐ 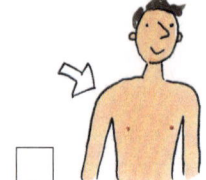 ☐ 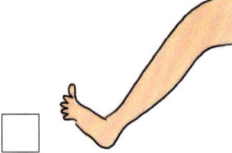 ☐  ☐

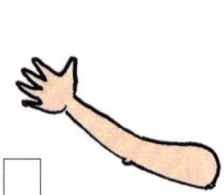 ☐ 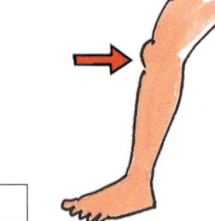 ☐ 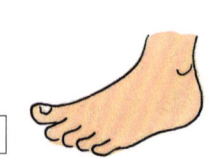 ☐

2 **Ich kann sagen, wie ich mich fühle:** ✔

Hilfe findest du im Activity Book auf den Seiten 11 und 12.

 ☐ I'm tired.    ☐ I'm happy.

 ☐ I'm sad.    ☐ I'm angry.    ☐ I'm scared.

Sally 3 Activity Book Förderheft (Englisch ab Klasse 1) © 2017 Cornelsen Verlag GmbH, Berlin